GRAYS THURROCK REVISITED

An engraving of Purfleet, published in 1832.

GRAYS THURROCK REVISITED

Barry Barnes

Phillimore

1991

Published by
PHILLIMORE & CO. LTD.
Shopwyke Hall, Chichester, Sussex

ISBN 0 85033 796 8

Printed and bound in Great Britain by
BIDDLES LTD.
Guildford, Surrey

Dedicated to the memory of Scamp. The best friend a man could ever have. He gave his all and asked for nothing.

List of Illustrations

Frontispiece: Purfleet, *c*.1832.

Introduction

After volume one of Grays Thurrock was published in June 1988 dozens of people asked me if or when I was going to do a second volume. I had not planned to do another book but such was the interest and demand that, thanks to my publishers and the people who pressed for it, here is volume two.

In the three and a half years since volume one was published, many changes have taken place in the area. Ford Place at South Ockendon was devasted by a fire and has deteriorated even further recently, as its front wall has blown down. It now looks as if the remains of this fine house, parts of which date back to the middle of the 17th century, will now be demolished to make way for a new building. After months of battling and legal wrangling by campaigners, the State Cinema in Grays was designated a listed building because of its superb 1930s decor. Opened on 5 September 1938, the building was used recently as a setting for film and television productions such as 'Bluebell', the story of the famous dancing troupe that was popular in the 1930s. After a change of ownership the cinema reopened and its future looked secure. Unfortunately the 'State' has closed again, partly because of the multi-screen cinema at the Lakeside Retail Park and is now (from 26 July 1991) being used as a venue for pop music concerts.

Much is happening in the way of redevelopment in Thurrock, not all for the good. Along the river front of Grays every available piece of land is being grabbed by developers and houses, some with boat moorings, are springing up. In the west the cement works around the *Wharf* Inn has been cleared away and the site is now another housing estate. In the east butting, right up against the grain terminal in Tilbury Docks, is another estate, occupying land where once was the Grays Co-operative bakery. Houses also cover the ground where Seabrooke's had their massive brewery, Grays Co-operative Society had its dairy and immaculate bowling green and Drums had their factory. Here also were once various jettys and yards, which are now given over to more houses.

The old High Street was cleared away a few years ago. With it went houses, shops and public houses, some dating back to the 17th century and earlier. This was an area laden down with history, an area which could have been preserved as a living museum, where small shopkeepers and tradesmen could have attracted many thousands of visitors if a far-sighted council or organisation had seen its potential. Kings Walk was built to replace the old High Street, and was designed to resemble the structures that once graced the area. Unfortunately the 20th-century plastic weatherboarding and other materials that were used in its construction produced a very poor imitation of their predecessors. This area is again being cleared as part of another 'redevelopment'.

Early in 1990 Joyes' old shops in New Road were replaced by civic offices. A few months earlier many of the shops on the opposite side of New Road to Joyes' store had also been demolished to make way for the new Town Hall. Businesses such as Emberson's Florists, Higgins's Printers, Bolton's Jewellers and Smith's Grocers are only a few who traded from the shops that have now gone.

Just outside Grays at the top of Hogg Lane on the site of an old rubbish dump, a World War Two anti-aircraft station and worked out chalkpits is the beginning of a 'new town', called Chafford Hundred. This project is to spread through the massive derelict quarries that lie between Hogg Lane and the giant Lakeside Retail Park that is adjacent to the M25 at Purfleet. During work on this site the habitat of countless birds, animals and plants was destroyed. Although a nature reserve is planned to be included, many badgers' setts were lost along with foxes and other smaller animals. In these quarries were colonies of rare wild orchids, but luckily many were saved by being transplanted to other secret sites. When completed Chafford Hundred will have about five thousand houses, and a school. A railway station will be built on the Grays to Upminster line, designed to service both the housing estate and the retail park. The second service station on the M25 opened not far from the retail park early in 1990.

Many plans have been put forward to develop vast areas of Thurrock in the future. Not long ago the possibility of a horse racing circuit on farm land on Orsett Heath was aired, while another plan is for a golf course and hotel on land adjacent to Tilbury Fort. It is also a possibility that the high-speed channel tunnel rail link will cross the Thames near Tilbury, the line running right through the heart of the borough. Yet another plan is for a massive multi-million pound rail terminal to be built at Tilbury. This would serve a suggested airport, which could be built on reclaimed land in the Thames Estuary.

By the time this book is published one very ambitious plan will have come to fruition, namely the third river crossing at Purfleet. The crossing will be the longest single-span suspension bridge in Europe and is set to become a landmark for miles around. It is planned to open in September 1991 to ease traffic congestion. The Queen will officially open and name the bridge on 30 October 1991.

Grays Thurrock has undergone enormous changes in the last 25 years. Much of the physical evidence of our past has gone. At the moment meetings are being held and plans are being drawn up for a whole new town centre in Grays, which it is hoped will revitalise the town. Only time will tell.

Unrest and Wartime

1.   Two years before the start of the Great War the Dock Strike of 1912 caused great excitement in Thurrock. Such was the unrest that soldiers and police had to be drafted in to quell any disturbances. The soldiers in this picture, thought to be Fusiliers, were photographed at Grays railway station during that strike.

2.   A fine picture taken at the time of the Dock Strike, this shows some more of the soldiers who were stationed here. They were camped in a field adjacent to Grays railway station goods yard. Note the policemen standing at the back and the sailor boys from one of the training ships seated at the front.

3. Mr. W. R. Menlove was perhaps the most prolific local photographer and was always quick to see an opportunity. In this photograph he was on the scene when a procession made its way down Grays High Street, at the time of the 1912 Dock Strike.

4. During the first few months after the start of World War One, Thurrock saw a lot of military activity. Having a main railway line running through the area and large docks it was an ideal mustering point. Taken by Mr. Menlove in 1914, this photograph has captured the 3rd Essex Battalion R. F. A., riding out of what is now the Territorial Army centre behind Brooke Road, Grays.

5. World War One caused excitement right across the country, and batches of 'Kitchener's Volunteers' departed with much ceremony. This photograph shows the band from the Training Ship *Exmouth* and relatives leaving Grays railway station after having seen off some local lads. In the centre background stands Mr. Harding's horse bus. This service ran between Orsett and Grays for many years early this century.

6. Another picture taken by Mr. Menlove in 1914, which has proved to be a valuable one. Not only does it show crowds of people waving off a train load of 'volunteers', but also a row of very fine houses that once lined Maidstone Road, Grays.

7. During World War One a large military camp was set up at Aveley. Few photographs exist to show us what it looked like. This photograph shows 'C. Company of the Buffs', and was taken at church parade in November 1914.

8. At Purfleet, just a couple of miles from Aveley, was a large garrison. Built at the end of the 18th century and conveniently placed alongside the river, its magazines could hold some 60,000 barrels of gunpowder. This picture shows the clock-tower as it looked *c*.1913. Most of the garrison site is now covered by a housing estate.

9. Kynochtown, a village and name that have now disappeared. Once a munitions factory, the site is today covered by oil refineries. During the war most employees at the munitions factory were women, either local or drafted in from all over the country. In this studio photograph, *c.*1916, five young ladies are dressed in their working overalls and hats. Each girl is wearing a triangular badge to signify she is employed in government work.

10. This snapshot was taken during World War One, and shows a Zeppelin following the Thames on its way to bomb London. The photograph is thought to have been taken *c.*1916 from a garden in Tilbury.

11.   During World War Two a Home Guard was set up and trained to protect the homeland against possible invasion. Sometimes only armed with broomsticks and home-made weapons, these men stood ready to repel the raiders that never came. The photograph above shows No.2 platoon, which was based at Aveley in 1942.

12.   After the war to end all wars, villages, towns and cities across the country set up memorials to commemorate those who had given their lives. Little Thurrock's war memorial stands at Turps Corner – named after a nearby farm – and was unveiled in 1922. This busy crossroads has also been called Polly Cook's corner, the name having come from a school that once stood nearby.

The Docks and River

13.   During times of unrest strategic points such as oil refineries and docks are heavily guarded. Tilbury Docks was no exception. This picture shows a detachment of territorials on guard in the docks, *c.*1915. Territorials were often used so that regular soldiers could be released for other duties.

14. Taken around 1910, this is an outstanding picture of the stern of the Training Ship *Cornwall*. It shows her mooring place in relation to the *Royal Hotel* at Purfleet.

15.   A study of some of the boys from the Training Ship *Exmouth*. These boys could often be seen attending various functions in the town, rowing between the shore and their ship, or taking part in exercises on the river. Here they are just about to leave their jetty for the crossing to the ship.

16.   Tilbury Docks has been operating now for over 100 years. Since its inception in 1886 it has grown to be one of the most important dockyards in Europe, if not the world. This photograph, taken in 1909, shows the workforce employed at the time by the London and India Dock Company, which was one of the many companies based there.

17.   A fine view of the new dry dock at Tilbury, *c*.1920, giving a good indication of just how enormous these docks are. Compare the height of the walls with the men on the floor of the dock. This dock was 110 ft. wide and 750 ft. long, and could be extended to 1,000 ft. The double row of mechanical bilge blocks was used to support the vessel when the water was drained out.

18. Aerial photographs are a valuable addition to any local history collection, as the photographer's bird's-eye position shows us so much. This picture, taken during the 1920s, reveals how busy Tilbury Docks were at the time. The Thames can be seen along the top, while in the bottom right can be seen the 'Dwellings' (blocks of houses) and the hair pin bridge

19. Many shipping companies have used Tilbury Docks, P. & O. is perhaps the one most can remember. This picture shows their 20,000 ton *Oronsay* being lined up by four tugs in readiness for her entry into the docks, *c*.1930.

20.   The Anglo American Oil Company (now Esso) built its works right alongside the banks of the Thames. The refinery at Purfleet, although greatly altered, is still working today. Some of the giant storage tanks and a ship tied up at the end of the jetty are shown here in 1920.

21.   In volume one of *Grays Thurrock and District* there was a picture of the S. S. *Iroquois* which, in the early years of this century, towed a barge known as the *Navahoe* across the Atlantic. The *Iroquois* and the *Navahoe* were transporting crude oil from the American oilfields to the Purfleet refinery. Here we see the *Navahoe* at Purfleet. The arrangement of six masts and sails was employed on the crossing when the wind allowed.

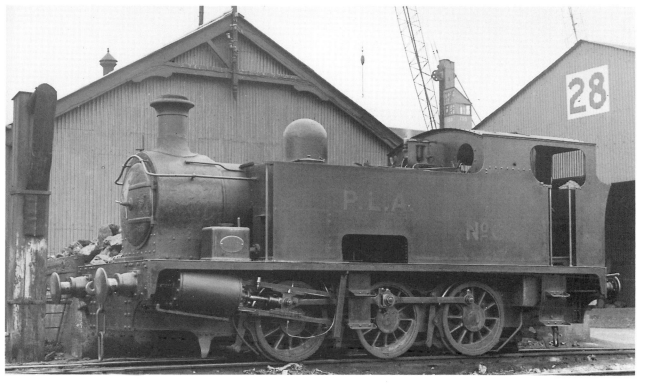

22. Many hundreds of miles of railway lines criss-crossed Tilbury Docks to facilitate the movement of cargoes. Here we see engine No.68, one of many engines that were used, c.1930. On the left of the picture can be seen the apparatus used to fill the engines' boilers with water. No. 28 shed is in the background.

23. Railways were used by quarries, factories and oil refineries as well as docks. Here a shunting engine is employed to haul tanks owned by the London and Thames Haven Oil Wharves Ltd., c.1920.

24. Thankfully accidents do not often happen on the Thames, but when they do there is usually someone around to record the event. Before photography was invented an artist would sketch or paint the scene; on this occasion a camera preserved an interesting occurrence. The date is unknown, but the postcard probably dates from the 1920s or '30s.

25. The *Gull* Lightship was stationed at many points around the British Isles during her long career. At one time she was holed in a collision and beached off Ramsgate in Kent. Used for many years as a club room by Thurrock Yacht Club, she now lies neglected and partly submerged in the mud of Grays foreshore.

26. Thurrock has long had associations with Thames Barges. This delightful picture shows three crew members posing on board the *Clara* whilst moored at Stanford-le-Hope wharf, *c.*1910. *Clara* was one of many barges owned by Ambrose Ellis of Stanford, and she came first in a barge race on the Medway in 1896.

Societies and Leisure

27. A rare photograph of Tilbury Constitutional Club, also known as the Blue House. It shows workmen proudly displaying the tools of their trade including a scythe, pickaxe, spade and hammer. Possibly the hall is decorated to celebrate the Coronation of George VI in 1937. Does anybody know why the workmen were posing like this?

28. This photograph shows what could have been the hierarchy of Tilbury Constitutional Club in the early 1900s. The club was situated in Broadway and, according to a sign in the window, was affiliated to the Association of Conservative Clubs.

29. A superb photograph taken at what is thought to be the back of the *Rising Sun*, High Street, Grays, *c*.1930. This public house is where the Exmouth Lodge of the Royal Antediluvian Order of Buffaloes held their meetings. Extreme left and right of group are Mr. and Mrs. Sims, longtime licensees of the *Sun*. Others known are Jack Going (3rd from left), Dorrington (4th from left), Gingall (2nd from right), Partridge (3rd from right) and Marchant (5th from right). Seated, left to right, are Cook, Barker and Hornsby.

30. This picture was taken in Tilbury and shows the stonelaying ceremony for the Wesleyan Church Hall, on 2 May 1928. The many children and babies in the crowd of onlookers indicate that Tilbury was still a growing town.

31. The Deneholes in Hangman's Woods, Little Thurrock, have long held a fascination for many people. For many years the shafts and chambers have been investigated, either by individuals or by organised groups, as seen here, *c.*1910. Essex Field Club was one organisation that arranged trips. So popular were these events that Seabrooke's Brewery set up a refreshment stall in the woods close to the Deneholes.

32. A popular leisure pursuit in the years before the First World War was cycling. All over the country local cycle clubs were set up, and in most towns and villages at least one 'cyclists' rest' could be found, to cater for them when out on the road. This picture shows the members of Grays Cycling Club *c.*1903. They are lined across Hogg Lane, Grays, when it was still a country lane. Note that each man is wearing his club badge on his cap. The man fifth from the left blew his bugle to warn other road users of the group's approach.

33. Another picture of Grays Cycling Club, taken *c*.1910. It shows them proudly posing outside the (now demolished) *Queens Hotel*, High Street, Grays, which was for many years their meeting place. Note the man on the right with a mandolin. He would probably have entertained the group while they were on excursions.

34. Hunting, shooting and fishing have always been favourite pursuits of the gentry. Here we have a wonderful photograph recording the end of a day's shooting, *c*.1910. I do not know the names of the men shown but they are posed in front of the *Dog and Partridge* at Orsett.

35. In the days before the private car made it easier for families to go away on holidays, employers arranged charabanc trips for their staff. Early this century the workforce was mostly men, so the outings were all-male events. This photograph, not the most professional but a marvellous record nonetheless, shows a group of local men on board a very early lorry cum charabanc, c.1910. The vehicle is called 'The Empress' and a plate on the side of the cab reads 'Downey. Jobmasters. Grays Essex'. A jobmaster was a livery stable keeper who had horses and carriages for hire.

36. This photograph is another example of Mr. Menlove's work. The group outside the *Theobald Arms*, Argent Street, Grays, is just about to set off for the 1914 Derby. One can only guess at how long it would have taken in this early open-top bus.

37. Another superb example of the all-male outing. This one is seen outside the *Club House* in London Road, West Thurrock (now the Shant). The date is unknown but they could have been celebrating a coronation: each man is wearing what could be red, white and blue rosettes. There are also black and white clowns on the front seat.

38. Public houses were popular departure and arrival points for outings. This group was about to leave the *Fox and Goose* in London Road, West Thurrock, in 1914, when Mr. Menlove preserved it for posterity.

39.   An unknown group who had their photograph taken by Edwin of Clarence Road, Grays, outside the *Kings Arms* in Baker Street, *c.*1920. The charabanc is a Daimler, and the band around the driver's straw boater reads 'Royal Sovereign'.

40. Purfleet Garrison Recreation Institute organised the annual outing that was photographed in 1922 by Edwin of Grays. This trip was clearly a family affair.

41. Many religious sects could be found in Thurrock in the late 19th and early 20th centuries. One such body can be seen here in this fine picture of the Zion Mission, *c.*1905, who held their meetings in Peartree Lane, Bulphan. Note the very severe mode of dress even for the youngest, and the portable harmonium.

GRAYS,
Y.P.
BAND.

42. Music has been a popular leisure pursuit throughout history. In some of the previous photographs men can be seen carrying 'squeeze-boxes' on their outings. Many factories and towns had their own bands, some of which went on to national fame. The Salvation Army in Grays recruited bandsmen at an early age. These young boys clearly enjoyed being in the Grays Y. P. (Young Persons') Band, pictured here *c.*1920.

43. This picture shows Grays Salvation Army's band, to which the youngsters seen in the previous picture could have graduated. The 'Sally' band has given many stirring performances over the years and given much pleasure and comfort to many people.

44. Much of Thurrock's shoreline was used as a beach by holidaymakers. Many Londoners made the journey, mostly by railway so that they could stay in the country. They stayed at resorts known to them as Purfleet on Thames, Grays Beach and, as we can see here, they enjoyed the beach at Stanford-le-Hope long before Southend became fashionable. This picture was taken *c*.1910.

45. Coronations, Jubilees, Royal Weddings and the end of war have always been good reasons for celebrating. Here we see a street party, which was held in Charles Street, Grays, probably to commemorate the Coronation of King George VI, in 1937.

Education

46.   Palmers School started in a small school room adjacent to Grays parish church around the beginning of the
18th century. This print, dated 1807, shows that early school room.

47. After moving to a site on the corner of the High Street and Orsett Road in the mid-1800s, the school moved to a new building on the corner of Chadwell Road and Southend Road in 1874. The following pictures show various aspects of that building. This is the south-east corner and shows what a fine imposing structure it was. Written on the reverse of this postcard of *c*.1903 is: 'We do enjoy ourselves in the dormitory, we have such fun...'.

48. From 1876 both boys and girls were educated at Palmers. In this picture of *c*.1920 we can see the girls' section, which was mainly on the eastern side. The girls stayed at the old school until 1931 when a new girls' school was opened a mile or so away, in Chadwell Road.

49. The headmaster's entrance, c.1911. It was situated on the south-west corner of the building, at the junction of Southend Road and Whitehall Lane, and directly opposite Palmers Avenue.

50. This is perhaps the best-known view of Palmers. The art and science block shown here was designed by Christoper Shiner, a local architect, and built by H. J. Carter of Grays, c.1900. It was demolished in 1980, and an old people's home and private houses now occupy the site.

51.   Amongst the many clubs and organisations set up within Palmers was a Cadet Force. This picture shows three of the smartly turned out lads from that force, c.1930. The Cadet Force was set up soon after World War One. Mr. Abbott, the headmaster, was appointed Cadet Lieutenant Colonel, and later became Cadet Colonel. During the summers of the 1920s camps were held at Southwold and Felixstowe. In 1931 the Cadet Force joined a national movement which trained recruits for the armed forces.

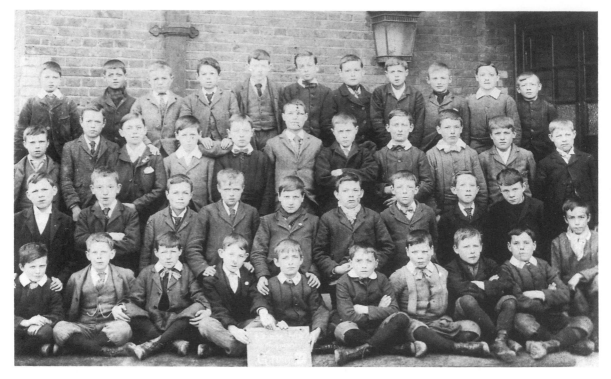

52. School groups have always been popular subjects for photographers, not necessarily because they liked children, but because there was a good chance that most of the children's parents would order a copy of it. In this picture, *c*.1890, we see the boys who attended Bridge Road School in Grays.

53. Here we have a mixed class of very young pupils who were at Quarry Hill School (now demolished) in Grays, *c*.1895. Note the carved wooden animals in the foreground.

54. Another picture taken at Quarry Hill School of a slightly older group and dating from around 1910. Note the stern expressions of both pupils and teachers.

55. Photographs of North Ockendon are hard to find. The date of this one is not known, but is possibly around 1910. Luckily somebody has written on the slate being held by the boy and girl, 'North Ockendon School, Group I'.

56. This picture, dated 1910, is thought to have been taken at Stanford-le-Hope School: the reason for the concert has been forgotten with the passing of time.

Belhus Mansion

Thurrock has had its fair share of visits from royalty and the nobility over the years. Elizabeth I made a famous speech here at the time of the Spanish Armada. King George VI came to Orsett when the Essex County Show was held there in 1948 and Elizabeth II and other members of the Royal Family have visited the area on a number of occasions. Nobility and the landed gentry have thought fit to live in the area for many years and a number of fine houses were built to accommodate them. In recent years a number of these houses have been lost: Belhus Mansion at Aveley, Belmont Castle at South Stifford and Ford Place at South Ockendon, which now stands a fire-ravaged ruin after mindless vandalism, are only a few. Some of these once grand houses are still standing to remind us of earlier times, for example, Coppid Hall and Stifford Lodge at North Stifford, and Orsett Hall. There are also many fine farmhouses in the area.

57. Belhus Mansion, parts of which could be traced back to the 16th century, was for many years the home of the Barrett-Lennards. During the First World War troops camped in its grounds. On the back of this postcard dated 1914 a soldier had written: 'Every morning we parade from 9.30 to 12.15 in front of the house, but at a great distance from it'. The camp would have been away to the right of the picture.

58. The Barrett-Lennards travelled in style. This coach was said to have been over 200 years old when it was photographed in the 1940s. It was decorated with panels of yellow ochre and upholstered in royal blue velvet. Seen with the coach is Mr. C. E. Osborne who was caretaker of the house for a number of years. The coach can now be seen in the Carriage Museum, Maidstone.

59. The interior of Belhus Mansion was absolutely magnificent. It contained some 84 rooms, many with heavily-carved panelled walls and elaborately-moulded ceilings. This photograph shows part of one of these rooms: the carved panels on the wall and chimney breast and the fine carved mantelpiece supports are visible. The fireplace and part of the panelling can now be seen in Thurrock Museum. The house was demolished in 1956.

Orsett Hall

Orsett Hall is one of the few remaining large country houses in the area, albeit now being used as an hotel and restaurant. The original house dates back to the early 17th century, and records show that it was greatly enlarged and rebuilt in brick for the Wingfield-Baker family in the 18th century. The ownership of the house passed to the Whitmore family, from Shropshire, in the late 1800s.

60.   This postcard print was produced in the 1920s. Although Orsett Hall is now used as an hotel, the grounds are largely unaltered from the time when the Whitmores lived there. In the lawn at the front of the house can still be found the gravestones of the family's much-loved dogs.

61. Captioned on the reverse of this print is 'Orsett, Stable Yard'. It is not known who the lady in the trap is, but she is possibly a young Lady Whitmore.

62. A rare photograph of Sir Francis Whitmore dressed in his hunting pink, taken at the start of a day's hunting on his estate, possibly before World War One. Sir Francis founded the Barstable Harriers, a pack of hounds that were kennelled behind the *Foxhound* public house in Orsett village.

63. A photograph taken in front of Orsett Hall between the wars. The occasion is not known, but four of the men have been identified. From left to right they are 1st, Mr. Ennis, Secretary of the Orsett Estate for many years; 6th, Mr. Germyne; 8th, Col. Sir Francis Whitmore; and 9th, the Earl of Athlone.

64. Another group photographed in front of the house, this time in the early 1950s and showing possibly the entire Whitmore family. In the middle of the front row is John Whitmore, who made quite a name for himself in British Saloon Car Racing a few years later.

65. The Whitmores were invited to Queen Elizabeth's Coronation in 1953. Here Sir Francis and Lady Whitmore are dressed in their finery for the occasion. The picture was used as a greetings card for Christmas 1953.

66. Sir Francis died aged 91 on 12 June 1962. This photograph shows his coffin being borne on a gun carriage on its way to Orsett parish church. In the background is the *Whitmore Arms* public house: the sign is draped in black as a mark of respect.

Fire and Police

Every community has cause to be grateful for its emergency services. Other than wartime when the emergency services in Thurrock played a marvellous part, the time of the East Coast floods was when their help was most needed. Many hundreds of locals were in debt to those men and women who worked day and night when the North Sea broke through the defences in February 1953. The photographs on the next few pages pay tribute to those who are there when we need them.

67. This studio photograph by Edwin of Grays serves as a record of the uniforms worn by members of the Grays Fire Brigade early this century.

68. Another fine posed photograph, by Smith of Grays. At the time possibly taken as a souvenir, it is a very important historical record showing as it does a splendidly turned-out engine and crew.

69. In 1903 the word 'Volunteer' was dropped from the Grays Fire Brigade, and the Urban District Council took over its running. This photograph, dated c.1926, shows members of the brigade with what is perhaps their new motorised fire engine at the back of the now-demolished fire station in Orsett Road, Grays.

70.   In the days when Thurrock was made up of local councils, a number of local fire brigades also operated. Grays Volunteer Fire Brigade had its headquarters behind the *King's Arms* in the High Street. In September 1890 a disastrous fire broke out in the *Queens Hotel*, which was attended by the Grays Brigade. The *Queens* was the pride and joy of Seabrooke and Sons, and was quickly rebuilt.

71. During the 1912 dock strike police officers were drafted in from all over the country. Here are seven stern-faced members of that team. They were photographed in the 'up-side' approach at Grays railway station.

ESSEX   SPECI
(Grays
ANNUAL   INSPEC

Special Constables   *Top Row*
Dann, Lee, Hall, Oakley, Robinson, Gibbs, Bridges, Newport, Robinson, Going, Gentgall, King, Chawner,

Special Constables   *Second Ro*
Pipes, Topsfield, Keeble, Warren, Collis, Titterington, Drinkall, Saveall, Shipman, Southgate, Carter, Ne

                                                                                                  Bottom Row - S.

Special Sergeants   *Special Inspector*   *Assistant Special*   *Special*

Quilter, Lott, Russell, Perry, Pavis.   *Franks*   *Chief Constable Capt. A. Royds*   *Genera*

72.   A photograph taken towards the end of World War Two, showing the Grays Division of the Essex Special Constabulary. Several well-known local names are mentioned in the list: for example, Going, Dines, Russell, Carter and Hall. Brick-built air raid shelters can be seen in the background.

CONSTABULARY
vision) —————
N 12th MARCH 1944

to Right.

e, Hazell, Nicholls, Merchant, Dines, Swallow, Benton, Scott, Hamblin, Blows, Stillaway, Owen, Latter.

ft to Right

ng, Moores, Marven, Walsh, Ward, Baker, Ford, Simmonds, Clarke, Stokes, Brightwell.

own - Left to Right

onstable   Special Superintendent   Superintendent   Special Inspector   Special Sergeants.

gemont   J. B. Chawner   E. H. Marriage   Fisher   Hockley, Reynolds, Wood
                                                                    Hawkins

73. At the end of the 19th century Tilbury had a rapidly growing population, and to administer law and order a police force had to be set up. This picture, from *c*.1910, shows just how large their headquarters in Dock Road were. The Tilbury police now operate from a new station in Civic Square.

74. The Victorians always favoured large impressive buildings for their civic offices. This is borne out by Grays police station. Built in Orsett Road, it had a commanding view of the High Street, but was replaced in the 1930s by a larger building on the same site. The second police station is now being used by the local courts.

Sport

All across the country villages, towns, cities, factories and public houses had their own sports teams. Most remained small and entertained on a purely local basis. On the next few pages we will see prime examples of Thurrock's contribution on this front.

75. Football teams tend to dominate any collection of sports photographs, so this one of Bulvan Cricket Club is a welcome exception. Dating from around 1908 it is the obligatory pre-match photograph.

76. Photographed outside the *Royal Hotel* at Purfleet. The board hanging from the railings proclaims they were the winners of the Grays and District First Division in 1903-4 and 1904-5. All the players have their winners' medals pinned to their shirts.

77. Originally known as Grays Juniors F.C., this team played on a ground known as the 'Hoppit' opposite the *Bull Inn*, Little Thurrock. Later they moved to the 'Lawn', also in Little Thurrock. In 1906 they moved to 'Grays Rec.' and changed their name to Grays Athletic F.C. Some of the teams that visited Grays in those early days were Catford, Barnet, Finchley, Luton and Southend. Back row and working clockwise: H. Smith (trainer), T. Blundell (linesman), J. Mason, A. Kempton, L. Banks, F. Jessop (secretary), T. Kelsey (committee). Middle row: J. Layzell, G. Gibbs, W. Nash (captain), H. Driscoll. Bottom row: H. Layzell, J. Woodgate, E. Appleford, P. Smith, J. Mullins (Vice-captain).

78. These are the Beaconstone Reserves in 1910-11. This is an example of a works team, as Beaconstone were builders' merchants in London Road, Grays. Back row second from right is Albert Whitby; middle row first left, Bill King; second left, Reg Knopp; first from right, Arthur Vaughan; second right, Ernie Hoath; front row first left, Sid Oakley.

79. More winners. Grays Melrose F. C. won the Grays Junior Cup in the 1918-19 season. Well-known local names appear again in the caption. At the extreme left of the middle row, H. Overall is wearing a sailor's uniform, a reminder that the Great War had only just finished.

80. A very keen-looking young team. These lads were based in West Thurrock and played for West Thurrock Juniors F. C. in the years just before World War One. The photograph was taken in the corner of West Thurrock recreation ground by Mr. Menlove of Grays.

81. Another happy local team, photographed by W. Harper of Tilbury. It is Lansdowne Road Old Boys, in about 1920. The team was formed up from ex-Lansdowne Road School pupils. Lansdowne Road School celebrated its centenary in 1991.

82.   This is how Grays Thurrock United F. C. looked in their 1928-9 season: they were possibly photographed at 'The Rec.'. In the line-up are two well-known local names, middle of centre row and sitting left foreground are the Boatman brothers. Back row: E. Wells (trainer), Morrison, F. Oliver (director), Alldridge, Pattison, Irvine, A. Rounce, G. Stamp (director). Centre row: W. Childs (chairman), Allen, Morgan, H. Boatman, Tredwell, Both. Front row: Boatman, Edwards.

83. It is not certain which team is pictured here, but it could be Grays Athletic F. C. in about 1948. All the players' names are known and some are quite amusing. Standing left to right: Dolly Lawson, Wah Wah Paddy, Belson Bairnfather, Chocca (slang for fed-up) Claydon, Ray Kemp, Pat (?)Nuth, Jack Gatenby, Whooper Stebbing and Big Horace. Kneeling in front: Vicar Graves, (?)Jumper Kettly, Harry Brand, Frank Rawkins and Tommy Manley. Seabrooke's Brewery is in the background.

Shops and Businesses

Grays Co-operative Society began in the Dutch House (see plate 170), Old High Street, Grays, in 1867. The following photographs show various aspects of its history. Some well-known local names were amongst the nucleus of those who started the society. They included George Turp, Henry Redington, Joseph Harris, Thomas Dines and John Snell.

84.   The next two photographs show one of the society's shops at the top of the Old High Street, Grays, opposite the market square. The sign on the front of the shop, in addition to advertising 'Home Killed Ox Beef & Wether Mutton', also promotes 'Prime Pickled Ox Tongues'.

85. The above photograph shows a group of workmen carrying out repairs to the shop, seen in the previous photograph, early this century. Even with this work going on the shop is still trading.

86. Just before the end of the 1900s Grays Co-op's second branch was opened in London Road, West Thurrock. This shop had both a grocery and butchery department. Note the glass-shaded gas lamps outside the shop.

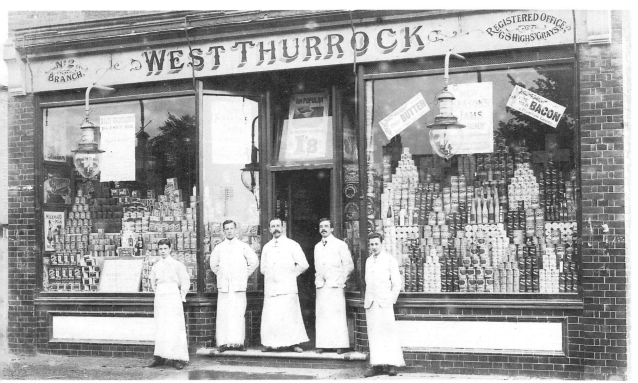

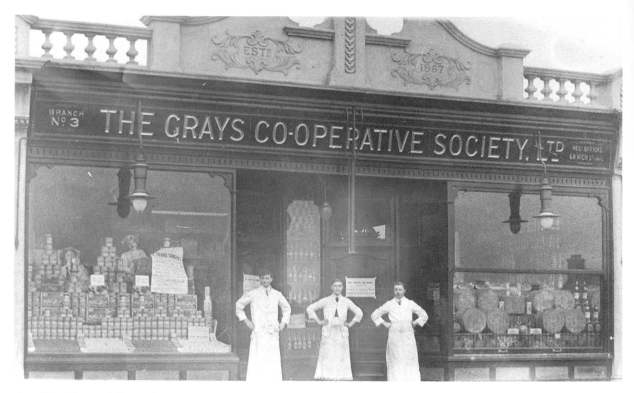

87. East Thurrock Road, Grays, was the site chosen for the Co-op's third shop. It was opened in 1903 at a time when the turnover of the company was more than £100,000, with a membership of four thousand.

88. Grays Co-op tried to cater for all. They sold the widest variety of goods from boots and shoes to paraffin, ran bakery and milk rounds, and had a greengrocer, butcher and draper as well as a grocer. To supply their shops with bread and confectionery, a bakery was built in 1897 close to the river at Grays. This photograph shows the first Thames Barge to arrive at the G. C. S. wharf loaded with wheat. The barge is the *Progress of Rochester*.

89. One of the Co-op's early horse-drawn bakery vans, No.1 of their fleet, which served the country areas.

90. A familiar sight and well-known name around Grays for many years was Bridger's Haulage. Charles Bridger operated his cartage business from Sherfield Road, Grays. His delivery wagon is seen here waiting outside Grays railway station during the 1920s.

91. Another local business no longer with us is Horncastle's, started by Charles Horncastle in the mid-1800s. Their first shop, shown here in 1845, was on the corner of High Street and New Road. Displayed outside are various linos and rugs, and small pieces of furniture.

92. The next two pictures show how Horncastle's expanded during the early 1900s. This shows the same shop as in the previous picture, but it has been dramatically increased in size, becoming Hosiers, Outfitters and Clothiers as well as Sea Outfitting Merchants.

93. Horncastle's second shop was just a few yards up New Road where, according to this photograph, everything including the kitchen sink could be bought. Some of the prices noted are: garden fork, 7s. 6d.; yard of chicken wire, 5½d.; set of three enamelled saucepans, 8s. 11d.; and set of three milk jugs, 4s. 9d. Horncastle's was taken over by William Perring in 1958.

94. For many years 'Birkenhall' was the home of Arthur E. Joyes, the founder of Joyes' store. Fine panoramic views of the Thames and Kent beyond could be had from the observation room on the roof of this house in Mill Lane, South Stifford.

95. Joyes' shop was in New Road. Founded about a hundred years ago, it was well known for its selection of quality goods, and for its annual sales, which attracted shoppers in their hundreds. This photograph shows the millinery department. Note the chairs against the counter for the use of female customers.

96. Printed from a glass negative, as was the previous one, this shows three of Joyes' delivery vehicles in front of the shop, c.1920. To the left of Joyes' shop is Frank West's second shop, opened in 1919, with Noad's beside that. Joyes' closed in the mid-1970s.

97. Just round the corner from New Road, at 74 High Street, was Bristow and Co., who traded as a Boot Warehouse and Seamen's Outfitters. This photograph was taken about 1890. The sign on the lamp post reads: 'In the interests of public health do not spit on the pavement'.

98. The High Street. Bristow's shop is visible again (taken over in 1913 by Frank West), and next door to Bristow's is the Clock Shop, run by A. W. Boatman. The Grays Co-operative Society's Central Store is on the end. The carts in the distance are waiting at the railway crossing.

99. Grays Market, when it was opposite the parish church, is fondly remembered for its selection of stalls and friendly atmosphere. One of the stalls was Going's 'cockle stall', on which all manner of 'fresh today' shellfish were offered. This picture of Jack Going was taken around 1917. The construction of Horncastle's new store can just be seen in the background.

100. Until recently there was a gentlemen's outfitters in Grays High Street named Westwood. In 1884 Charles Westwood opened his first shop at No.26. The business soon flourished and outgrew the shop.

101. About 1905, Westwood's moved to this shop, a few yards along the High Street at No. 62. The business stayed here until it closed down in the 1980s. Westwood's was an agent for Palmers School uniforms.

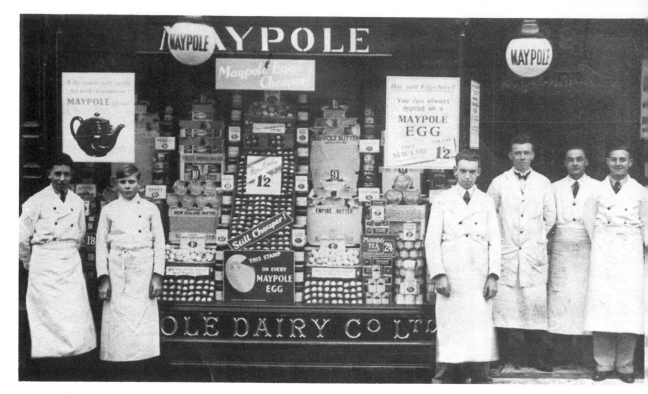

102.   This photograph, taken during the inter-war years, shows the premises of the Maypole Dairy Company at 29 High Street, Grays. This shop is still remembered by many older residents for its old style of service and its excellent selection of cheeses and bacon.

103.   Butchers are very proud of their profession and go to great trouble to make a good display. Osborn's shop in Clarence Road, Grays, was included in Vol. 1. but this is a different view, and those photographed are named. From the left Lennard Osborn (youngest brother), Ernie Osborn (brother), Ethel Osborn (sister), Charles Osborn Jnr., Emily Osborn (mother) and Charles Osborn (father).

104. Gryll's radio shop in Clarence Road, Grays, as it looked in the 1940s. It is now Unwin's car spares. Most of the popular makes of radio were stocked here including Pye, Ekco and Marconiphone.

105. Almost opposite Gryll's shop was a butcher's shop, said by many to be the best in Grays. Mr. Munt, seen here in the doorway of this shop, died a few years ago. The shop has been demolished, but the business is still in existence, run by Mr. Munt's son, Robert.

106. Another well-known family butcher's shop. This is how A. Johnson and Son's shop in William Street, Grays, looked in about 1899. The business was started in Queen Victoria's reign by Abraham Johnson. On the extreme left and right are brothers David and Albert. The lady on the left is the wife of Abraham Johnson, and David Johnson's wife is wearing the white dress.

107. This snapshot was found in an envelope containing scraps of paper and shop receipts at a jumble sale. It shows two members of the Thurrock butchery business of J. W. Hart and Son, possibly during the 1920s. Unfortunately the names of the men or where the picture was taken are not known.

108. Another butcher no longer trading is Jim
Cutts, of London Road, West Thurrock.
Situated on the end of a short row of shops (now
demolished) opposite the *Ship* public house, it
had its own slaughterhouse at the rear. This
picture was taken just before Christmas in the
early 1920s and shows Jim Cutts on the right.
Tom Ayden is holding the cow.

109. Not far from Jim Cutts' shop was this one,
known as Polley's. Mrs. Polley is thought to be
the lady in the doorway. The shop, now a house,
was almost opposite the Magnet works. The
poster in the window is announcing a 'Special
Meeting, Whit Monday in West Thurrock
Gospel Hall'.

110.   The east side of South Road, South Ockendon, remains largely unaltered as we can see from the next two pictures. Looking towards the village green, the building in the foreground was Wright's Butchers and is still a butcher's shop today. The half-weatherboarded houses have been converted into shops since this picture was taken early this century.

111.   This is the same row of shops shown in the previous picture, but viewed from the opposite end. Poulter's shop is now a chemist. Extreme right is Ockendon Stores, and in the centre is Cast's baker's shop.

112.   Today we expect post offices to be well appointed and easily accessible. The fence at Bulphan's post office in the years just before World War One looks more like a barricade to keep customers out. A Victorian post box is to the right of centre and, according to the signs, one could buy Nestlés Milk, Bovril, Sunlight Soap and Ceylindo Tea in the shop.

113.   Every town had its quota of tradesmen. Some retailed through shops, others used yards and workshops. This photograph shows two local tradesmen who found it viable to share the same premises in Sherfield Road, Grays. At the back of the yard one of Seabrooke's delivery drays is being repaired.

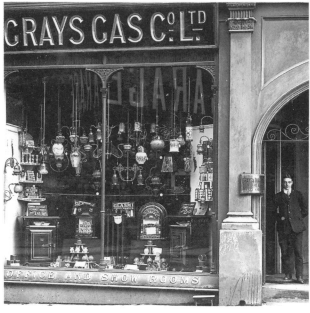

114. In the early days of heat and light supply, the distribution was organised on a purely local level. The Grays and Tilbury Gas Company was a household name. Here we have three pictures concerning the company. This shows their offices and showrooms in Orsett Road, Grays (now council offices).

115. Another of the company's shops was in Grays High Street, between the Empire Theatre and the railway crossing. In the window, in addition to the fires, lamp fittings, shades and mantels, a showcard advertises that a Cannon gas cooker can be rented for 1s. 6d. per quarter.

116. A superb picture of four young men employed by the Grays and Tilbury Gas Company in about 1920. It is possible that they were meter readers and emptiers, and the chap with the barrow would have been employed to pick up the money from them.

117.   Wharf Road, Stanford-le Hope. The first building on the right-hand side is the shop of Herbert John Bewers. The sign on the end wall shows that he traded as 'H. J. Bewers. Cash Stores. Stationer and Confectioner, glass, china, earthenware and general provision merchant'.

118.   In the years before World War One when this and the previous photograph were taken, private and public transport were virtually non-existent. To combat this many shops operated a delivery service, and here can be seen the delivery van used by Bewers of Wharf Road, Stanford-le-Hope.

119.   We are very lucky that somebody thought it necessary to write the following on the back of this photograph: 'Timothy White's and Taylors. Branch Pharmacy. Stanford-le-Hope, Essex. July 1936. Relief dispenser for 3 weeks'. Without this information it could have been a picture of a shop anywhere in the country.

120. Industry has been in Thurrock in one form or another since earliest times. In South Stifford, Wouldhams built a massive cement works. The works were built to process the thousands of tons of chalk and other raw materials coming from the enormous pits being dug in the area. This picture shows the sprawl of the factory, while in the foreground are some of the diggings and spoil heaps.

121. The next few pictures date back to the early years of Thurrock's cement industry. Although not in good condition, this is a rare and important picture (below). It shows the offices of the Grays Chalk Quarries Co. Ltd. in about 1890. We can see the management (in top hats), the office staff and some of the workmen.

122. In the centre of this picture, a man can be seen holding one of the tools of his trade namely the iron pole with a ring handle. The man standing fourth from left could be a driver, as slung around his neck is a short plaited whip, for urging the wagon horses.

123. A local quarry, pictured early this century. The man standing in the chalk 'chimney' would use the iron tool to dislodge chalk, which would then fall into the wagons below.

124.   For many years railway lines have been an ideal means of moving heavy loads. In the various works and quarries across Thurrock many hundreds of miles of steel rails have been laid. The engine seen in this photograph was named 'Albert' and was owned by Thurrock Chalk and Whiting Company.

125.   This strange-looking vehicle was called 'Goliath', and was employed for many years by the Alpha Cement Company of West Thurrock.

126. Flint's is a name long associated with Thurrock. Their shop in Orsett Road, Grays, is now closed. Over the years they sold cycles, D.I.Y. sundries and hobby materials, as well as being a holiday and coach booking agent.

127. During the early years of the wireless Flint's was a pioneer. This photograph was taken at the Orsett Show during the 1930s, when Flint's set up the public address system. Their delivery van was a familiar sight around the area for many years.

128.   In volume one there is a picture of Reddington's lorry at the rear of their shop. Here is a picture of that shop at 12 High Street, Grays. It shows a First Prize winning display. We do not know what year it was, but judging from the fact that holly and mistletoe are present it is near Christmas, perhaps in the 1920s.

129. Seabrooke and Sons' Thurrock Brewery has been mentioned already. Taken over by Charringtons in 1929, they once owned or supplied nearly every public house in Thurrock, and their delivery vans were frequently seen. This fine example was built by Commercial Cars and is seen here outside the brewery c. 1910. Note the chain-driven rear wheels.

130. Before petrol engines, horses were used to pull the drays and wagons. Seabrooke's had workshops for building and repair, and this remarkable indoor photograph shows that workshop and some of the craftsmen employed there.

131. Seabrooke's had other interests in addition to brewing, one of them being the supply of coal. Pictured here with the brewery in the background is one of their delivery carts.

132.   Motoring in its many aspects has employed many Thurrock people over the years. One of the first local garages was on the A13 at Purfleet. This rather faded snapshot of Painter's Garage shows petrol pumps with swing-out arms: cars stopped on the roadside then. Painter's was an agent for Pratts, B.P., Redline and Castrol. A garage still occupies the site.

133.   Stacey's Garage in London Road, Stanford-le-Hope, has a less jumbled appearance. They were agents for Shell, National and B.P. petrol at 1s. 4d. per gallon, B.S.A., Raleigh and Hercules pushbikes, A.J.S. motorbikes, H.M.V. gramophones and records, Mazda valves and Dunlop tyres. They also repaired gramophones, recharged accumulators, and sold Morris and Wolseley cars. The car on the right is for sale at £46.

134. This is how Daneholes Garage looked in the early 1950s. Built on the site of an old farm on the A13 (now A1013) at Little Thurrock, the dark wooden buildings at the back were once part of the original farm buildings, and are being used to garage cars.

135. The officers of Grays Working Men's Social Club and Institute, photographed in 1911 by Alfred Russell of Grays.

Transport

136.   For over a hundred years Tilbury has had a busy dock. Many thousands of ships, from tramp steamers to luxury liners, have called here. Much business has been generated by the docks, and local firms have taken advantage of it. One of those firms was the Tilbury Laundry Co. Ltd. whose premises were in Ferry Road and Dock Road.

137.   Although soft drinks manufacturers, Knowles, closed down in December 1977, they still remain in the memory for their quality and variety. This picture, taken at the time when they were amalgamated with Tampkins, shows left to right sitting Bert Wilson, George Thompson, Leon Knowles and Tampkins Jnr. Standing are Tom Tampkins, Ambrose Knowles and Mr. Judd.

138.   Another superb photograph by Edwin of Grays, it shows how petrol engines were taking over from horses. These delivery vans belonged to J. W. Pigg and Sons and are lined up outside their shop and bakery in Rectory Road, Orsett, in the early 1930s. The names of some of those shown are Kimmings, Redgewell, Keeling, Wright, Dorrington and Goodrum.

139. The vehicle pictured here once served a very important function, and was known locally as the Smallpox wagon. Within living memory Thurrock had an isolation hospital for contagious diseases in Long Lane Grays. The Smallpox wagon is standing in front of one of the hospital wards, about fifty years ago.

140. Buses have always proved to be a popular and reasonably cheap form of transport. Many private operators ran regular services across the area during the first decades of this century. In West Thurrock the Clarke family had three buses, one of which was horse drawn. Here we see that horse bus. Mrs. Clarke is the lady wearing a large hat and sitting above the driving lamp; Mr. Clarke is to her right. The horses were called Gert and Daisy.

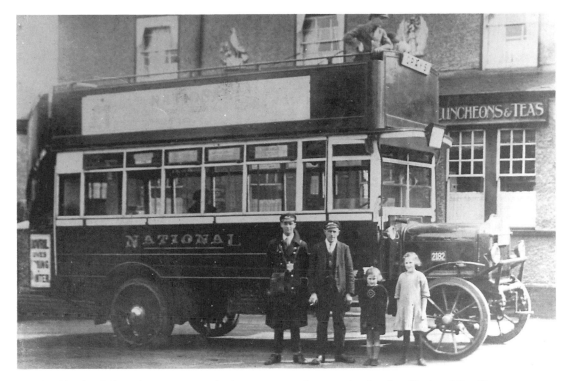

141. Slowly all the private operators in the area were taken over by the giant National Bus Company. This photograph c.1920 shows a wonderful solid rubber-tyred open-top bus belonging to that company. Photographed outside the *Whitmore Arms* in Orsett, its destination board indicates it was en route to Grays.

142. It seems that, whenever somebody turned up with a camera, people would collect to be photographed. Captured on film here is a happy band of drivers, conductors, inspectors and 'grease monkeys'. They were photographed outside the bus garage when it was in Argent Street, Grays. In the background can be seen a 'modern' closed-in single decker and to the right is an older open-top double decker.

143.   George Everitt Carter had a shop in Grays High Street from about 1905 catering for the new motoring craze. He was one of the first businesses in Thurrock to build and sell motor cars, and must also have been one of the first to hire out vehicles for weddings and funerals.

144.   One of a number of snapshots found in an old shoe box, this shows Tommy Topple in what is thought to be a De Dion. He is seen in Bridge Road, beside Grays Park, before World War One. Tommy was apprenticed to Carter's Garage and after the war he ran a cycle hire shop in Stanley Road. He also had a black Daimler, which he used for weddings and funerals.

145.   Corringham Light Railway was built to carry workers to Kynoch's explosives factory. The 2¾-mile line was opened in 1901, with a station at Corringham. This is a picture of one of their engines at Corringham Station: the Avonside 0-6-0ST was built in 1917 and worked until the railway closed on 1 March 1952. The engine was scrapped in 1957.

146.   This wonderful photograph is thought to have been taken during the 1920s. It shows a gang of council workmen in Clarence Road, Grays, with all the necessary equipment for road repairs.

General Views

147.   This superb picture shows Stifford Road as it leaves Baker Street. In the distance is the *King's Arms*. The row of six thatched cottages, known as Mill Cottages, were demolished about 20 years ago. Mill House, to their left, dates back to the 17th century and was once a cyclists' rest.

148.   This is how Orsett village looked in the winter of 1907. The cottages shown here once graced the High Road, next to the village butcher's, now closed down. A bus stop and meeting hall now occupy the site.

149.   A photograph taken around the beginning of the century shows more of Orsett High Road. On the left is the *Swan Inn*, now the site of the *Foxhound*. The large weatherboarded house next to the *Swan* was destroyed in a fire. The canopy in the distance on the right marks the village butcher's.

150.   These pretty cottages, built mainly in the 17th century with a 16th-century cross wing, can still be seen today in Orsett village, next to the *Whitmore Arms*.

151.   Hall Farm, parts of which date back 400 years, stands at the bottom of Pound Lane, Orsett. The traditional site of Bishop Bonner's Palace is a few yards to the north of the farmhouse.

152. Postcard views of East Tilbury are rare: this one shows the village street from the south. On the right is a row of newly-built council houses, on the left is the 'old' *Ship Inn*. The now-demolished village school can just be seen on the left in the distance.

153. This photograph of East Tilbury church is dated 1858. It shows the wooden spire and belfry, which were removed in 1906 during restoration and never replaced.

154. A quiet country lane at Orsett as it was about seventy years ago. Now much widened, and classed as the A128, it links the busy A13 and A127 trunk roads. Golding Bridge was roughly where the white posts are and was until quite recently just a slight bump in the road is derived from a family called Goldyng who once lived in the parish.

155. Linford was once called Muckingford. The name was changed in the 19th century when a since-aborted development was planned. There are few visible links with the past. This pre-First World War picture shows the old *George and Dragon* public house when it was owned by Seabrooke and Sons.

156. A hundred years ago most villages in this area had at least one windmill. The windmill at Horndon on the Hill stood close to the church until about 1917. The mill field is now covered by houses, although the ruins of the mill's roundhouse still remain.

157. To the south of Horndon is the hamlet of Pump Street where once stood the pump that supplied water to the village on the hill. This picture taken *c*.1910 shows what a splendid pump it was. The girl holding the handle is thought to be Jessie Bibby, aged 12 years.

158. The houses that made up the hamlet of Pump Street, photographed *c*.1915. Many of them still stand today. The pump seen in the previous picture stood on the right-hand side of the road opposite the houses.

159.   Fobbing is a delightful and mostly unspoilt village which still retains many relics from its past. This view looking north along the High Road shows the village stores once run by Mrs. Halston and now Hurst's builders' supplies. The brick-built house is Prosbus Hall which dates from the 16th century, and has 18th-century alterations.

160.   On the northern side of Fobbing, where the road heads out towards the Vange *Five Bells*, there stand Fishers Cottages. These cottages date back some five hundred years. Alterations have been made over the years in an attempt to make them more habitable but they still have all of their old world charm.

161. Daneholes Roundabout is a well-known landmark. This is how it looked at about the time of the First World War. The road the bus is coming down is from Stanford-le-Hope. Hangmans Wood, where the Deneholes are, is in the centre of the picture. The gate the man is sitting on was the entrance to a farm, which is now Daneholes Garage.

162. Dock Road, Little Thurrock, *c.*1910. In the centre of the picture is the *Bull Inn*, which was built over 200 years ago alongside the Brentwood to Tilbury Fort stage-coach route. During renovation work a few years ago wooden beams that were once ships' timbers were discovered.

163.   A busy scene in Dock Road, Tilbury, near the town railway station. The reason for the activity is unknown, but it could be a meeting during the 1912 Dock Strike.

164. A photograph taken in North Road, South Ockendon, some 90 years ago, which shows what had to be demolished to make way for Pear Tree Close and a row of new shops. The lady in a white dress is standing in the doorway of the village bicycle shop.

165. South Ockendon village has lost many of its old buildings. The west side of the High Street (now South Road), shown here, has all gone. Just left of centre, next to the weatherboarded cottages, the old *King's Head* can just be seen.

166.   Fobbing Road, Corringham, *c.*1910. The large brick building, built for Seabrooke's Brewery, was at this time the *Dukes Head* public house and off licence. It has also been the village shop. The delivery cart belonged to Bewers of Wharf Road, Stanford-le-Hope.

167. Aveley's High Street has been greatly altered, and the next two pictures show how it looked early this century. This is the lower end. Ship Lane enters on the left just beyond the horse and cart; the houses in the foreground are now shops.

168. The top end of Aveley High Street. In the distance on the right is Mill Lane. The houses on the left have now been replaced by shops.

169. Orsett Road, Grays, when the pace of life was a little more leisurely. In this parade of shops there are, from the left, Green's post office, unknown, Crussell's butcher's, Noad's music shop (formerly White's), and Hubbard's greengrocer's.

170. Grays Co-operative Society's first shop was the Dutch House in Old High Street, Grays. Built in typical Dutch style, parts of it could be traced back to the 17th century. The building was used by the society for three years from 1867. It was demolished in 1950.

171.   Further down the Old High Street was the *Anchor and Hope*. Dating back some 300 years, stories abounded about this public house's connections with smugglers. Alas, the whole of this area was cleared away a few years ago.

172. A day off school for these children seen in High Street, Stanford-le-Hope, *c*.1915. The shopping precinct has replaced the timber houses to the right of centre. John E. Green's draper's shop is at the end of the row.

173. The work of local photographers has been invaluable in the compilation of this book and its predecessor. To end with, a publicity photograph of the much-mentioned W. R. Menlove, taken about 1920.